AF445276

He Leaves the Ninety-Nine

First paperback edition April 2026

ISBN 979-8-9955467-0-2 (paperback)

Cover art by Molly Weidenfeller

gracewrites2001@gmail.com

To my dear family, each and every one of you,
thank you for being a place of comfort and
love. To God be the glory.

Contents

He Leaves the Ninety-Nine

"Suppose one of you has a hundred sheep and loses one of them. Doesn't he leave the ninety-nine in the open country and go after the lost sheep until he finds it? And when he finds it, he joyfully puts it on his shoulders and goes home. Then he calls his friends and neighbors together and says, 'Rejoice with me; I have found my lost sheep.' I tell you that in the same way there will be more rejoicing in heaven over one sinner who repents than over ninety-nine righteous persons who do not need to repent."

~ Luke 15:4-7 NIV ~

You are Welcome Here
- Introduction -

"Come to me, all you who are weary and burdened, and I will give you rest. Take my yoke upon you and learn from me, for I am gentle and humble in heart, and you will find rest for your souls. For my yoke is easy and my burden is light."
~ Matthew 11:28-30 NIV ~

Welcome, and thank you so much for joining me on a journey through the beginning of my story in the form of 15 devotionals! I am so grateful for you.

For those who don't know me well—or at all—my name is Grace, or Gracie, Hockin. I was born in Michigan to two amazing parents, grew up with two of the best older siblings a kid could ask for, and now I'm married to the husband God prepared for me. Because of them—and my other dear family and friends—and their prayers of intercession for me, I am still alive today and was able to run back into the arms of God, finally finding *home.* Everything I have and everything I am today is thanks to God's mighty power to save, restore, and redeem. I know beyond a shadow of doubt that without God, I would have lived in sin and mental agony until it rotted away at my heart, pushing me to give up on living any longer. There were times it came close to that, but God wasn't done writing my story yet, and I'm so, so thankful for that.

My relationship with God was not straightforward and simple. It was many nights of crying out to be healed, being in so much shame that I avoided praying so I wouldn't have to face God, and questioning everything, even so far as to doubt if the Bible was the word of God. There were days that I believed I had messed up too many times to be allowed to go back to him. That I was a dirty hypocrite unworthy to be called his child. Because when I gave up on myself, I was convinced that he would too. But he didn't. He never did, and he never will. Our Father in heaven is not scared of our doubts, our questions, or our misplaced anger towards him. Instead, he continuously searched for me, rescued me, loved me, and patiently waited for me to return home with him to find my rest—my peace—in his arms.

Now that I've asked him to be the savior of my life, he heals my heart daily, and I experience peace and joy that truly shouldn't exist within me. Jesus makes that possible. Jesus is the only way. Even if you are not on board with all this Jesus stuff, please, please, please keep reading. Because maybe my experience will help you see God in a new light. Maybe you will finally know peace, too.

I pray that, while reading my story, you won't feel alone as you walk through your own; that you will feel seen, loved, and hopeful once more. I pray that God will speak to you through the lessons and trials I experienced so that you will find the fire escape much sooner than I did. I pray that you find peace and rest in the arms of God. I pray that you come *home*.

You are so loved on Earth and in Heaven.

The Depths of God's Love
- Day One -

"For God so loved the world that he gave his one and only Son, that whoever believes in him shall not perish but have eternal life. For God did not send his Son into the world to condemn the world, but to save the world through him."
~ John 3:16-17 NIV ~

When I was in the classic stage of thinking that all of my problems were because of God, I tried to find every possible way to show that he wasn't actually a loving and kind father. I was angry that I had to suffer and hurt when I thought I was a decent person that didn't deserve it, and naturally—at least in my head—I believed that God didn't actually love me because of my circumstances. So I searched the Bible to find that one thing I could bring to God and say, "Look, I was right. You don't love me, and it's your fault I'm hurting."

My search was actually quite easy; with little effort, I found the place where I believed God slipped up and showed his true colors. Growing up in a Christian home, I knew very well the story of Jesus, and how God the Father sent him to

Earth to die for our sins as the perfect and holy sacrifice to bridge the gap between God and us so that we can have eternity with him; and this was the very story I latched onto. I went to God with a smug smile, saying, "God, if you really loved me, you wouldn't have sent your son to die; you would have come down yourself and died for me." I thought I was so smart and that I had found the reason I could blame God for my pain guilt-free. But that only lasted a few seconds. God spoke to my heart, and I was instantly humbled, heartbroken for God, and so thankful for his love.

He said to me, "Would you die for someone you love?" and I thought to myself that I would even die for a stranger if they needed help. Then he said, "Would you send your mom to die for a stranger that hates you? Would you send your sister? Your brother? Your father? Your future child?"

I began to weep.

I finally understood the true sacrifice of Jesus' death. It wasn't just Jesus who paid the price for sins. God the Father had to send his only Son to a world that hated him, and while Jesus prayed and cried in the garden for this burden to be taken from him (Luke 22:42 NIV), God had to say no, all because God loves us so much and wants to restore us to himself. I can't imagine what that was like. I can't imagine that kind of love.

In that same moment of realizing how painfully wrong I was to doubt God's love, I was also reminded where the blame truly lay: Satan. When sin entered this world through Satan's temptation and humans' free will in the garden, Earth became a fallen world, meaning bad things happen because Satan lives here and rules over many hearts. The horrible things I've experienced are because we live in a fallen, broken world in need of a savior; because humans have free will, and some of them used it to do evil things against me. But that's exactly why God sent his son. To save us. To save us from ourselves, from Satan, from a groaning world full of disease and natural disasters, and to create the way to Heaven—a place without scars, sin, suffering, or anything else that doesn't bring glory to God. So the blame is not on God. My anger should not be directed at his outstretched hand, waiting for me to take it and find rest. My blame, anger, and disgust should all be pointed towards Satan. He is the one who hurt you. He is the one who deceived you into thinking it was God. He was the one who worked so hard to make you believe he doesn't even exist, or even worse, that God doesn't exist. If that is where you are in your story, please read the next devotional and hear how Satan became painfully real to me.

You are so loved on Earth and in Heaven.

Spiritual Warfare
- Day Two -

"For our struggle is not against flesh and
blood, but against the rulers, against the
authorities, against the powers of this dark
world and against the spiritual forces of evil in
the heavenly realms."
~ Ephesians 6:12 NIV ~

When I was 12 years old, I stayed up late with my sister, fantasizing about our future. We giggled about the type of person we would marry, what career we would have, and anything and everything else young girls dream up. But then, something unexpected happened. As if they weren't my own words, I started saying what our futures would hold with a level of confidence and authority that made us think it must be God speaking through me, telling us everything we ever wanted, promising us exactly what we hoped for. Once the supernatural experience paused, we both marveled at how God must have come down to use me as a bringer of good news. Then it began again. My sister asked questions, and I—*it*—answered without hesitation. She asked, "Are you the

Lord?" (She had wanted to ask if it was God, but her throat closed up when she tried, but "lord" could come out). The reply was, "Yes." And in that moment, I felt compelled to reach down from my top bunk and hold her hand. She later told me that the hand she held wasn't my own. It was bigger, stronger, harrier, and obviously the hand of a man. As the supernatural experience came to a close, the spirit said not to tell our brother, dad, or pastor about the encounter since they wouldn't understand. So we agreed. We didn't share this miraculous experience of prophesying with anyone.

I began praying aloud much more and thought it felt more "intimate" not to say "In Jesus' name, amen," or really say his name at all. I would just speak aloud as if I were talking to another person in the room. I thought my relationship with God was deepening, and maybe I would start to find relief from the daily war that raged in my head. I was naive and weak-minded due to other things in my story, which I will detail a little later.

One afternoon, while we were hanging out with our mom, we felt compelled to tell her what had happened. We told her the whole account with wonder in our eyes, truly still believing it was God. We also made sure to ask that she keep this between us, as the spirit instructed, but little did we know that my brother had been eavesdropping the whole time and had shared the supernatural experience with our dad! At the time, I would have been so angry knowing what he did, but now, I am so thankful.

About a week later, my dad wanted to have a heart-to-heart with the family to go over entertainment that was beginning to concern him as he saw our attitudes (mostly mine) change in a negative direction. While we listened and discussed what God was calling us to give up, I felt that same feeling I did in the bedroom and opened my mouth to speak. (Even now I shake as I write this.) I declared with an authority I had never had before, claiming that God was telling me we shouldn't listen to dad and that we should indulge in what makes us happy. But my father, being a strong man of God, told me, "You are using God's name to do what you want to do, not what he wants." Immediately, an all-consuming sense of fear and dread filled my body, and everything in me screamed to get away from Dad! As he stepped closer to see what was wrong, I cried, "Stay away! Get away from me! You're scaring me! You're hurting me!" and practically tried to dig through the flooring to get away from him even though he wasn't touching me, or raising his voice. At this point, my spirit had taken a back seat, and I was viewing the interaction from a third-person standpoint (which I personally think points to the fact that I have a soul since I left my body), watching as I was truly terrified of Dad—of the Holy Spirit within him. My brother and dad said that when I looked up, my eyes were completely black, demonically dark, not just my pupil dilating to cover my irises, the whole eye—even with just a quick internet search, you will learn it is not scientifically possible, which means the only explanation is supernatural. I think it's also important to point out that both my dad and my brother saw my eyes like that, so it wasn't just my dad going through psychosis and hallucinating my eyes to be black because of the intense situation he was in. Also, when I was looking up at them, I was underneath a ceiling light that shone down on my face, so they could see my eyes very clearly. I wish I could recall everything that happened in the next few moments, but the only thing I'm certain of is that my dad was shocked and worried for me—along with everyone else—and sought God's help.

The next thing I remember, when I was back in the driver's seat of my body, was talking with my sister in our room, wrestling with what happened, and coming to terms with the fact that it was not God; it was a demon. Once I declared that it was not God, it left.

My brother remembers waiting in the kitchen—while I was still talking with my sister—trying to rationalize what happened, and suddenly being overcome with a need to pray.

He listened and began praying for safety and protection, and as he did so, he watched a translucent, shimmery humanoid figure move through the room and out the door, bringing with it coldness and fear.

That was the day I was delivered from demonic possession.

Unfortunately, this is not my family's only encounter with the unseen evil in the world. My brother has many stories of entities speaking to him, staring down a hall engulfed in a black void while a dog barked at the darkness with its tail tucked, and many other strange experiences. Seriously, just ask my dad, brother, and other members of my family; they will assure you that we are, in fact, living in a world with demons.

After that terrifying experience, I spent almost a decade of my life being scared of it happening again. I lived with so much sin, shame, fear, and anger, but didn't want to go to God for help, worrying I would find something else.

But God wasn't going to leave me there.

In the last couple of years, I found a podcast that started to shift my perspective and calm my fear. It's called "Haunted Cosmos" by Ben Garrett and Brian Sauvé. These two Christian men shine a light into the darkest parts of the world and bring them into a Biblical perspective. Although some of the episodes were genuinely terrifying, they helped me understand more about how Satan works and the extent of the evil in this world, and I began to find comfort in learning their patterns and how to safeguard myself. I learned that most demonic forces need permission to enter, and that Jesus' name truly casts them out, just like the Bible teaches us. I discovered the real reason why there was a demonic spirit in our home in the first place—which is not my story to tell—and it gave me clarity as to what happened and how to avoid it. I gained a deeper understanding of what Satan tells us vs. what God tells us, so I began praying that the Holy Spirit would gift me with discernment and peace so that I could step into a full relationship with Christ without fear, with clear eyes, and God did just that.

As I grew in my faith, I discovered that many sins are tied to real, demonic spirits that want to pull you away from God through temptation, which makes those sins much harder to stop and repent. That's why Peter warns us to be aware at all times for Satan's attacks.

"Be alert and of sober mind. Your enemy the
devil prowls around like a roaring lion looking
for someone to devour."
~ 1 Peter 5:8 NIV ~

I will go into further explanation of my new take on sin and temptation, and how I overcame it, in a later devotional. But now that you know why I believe Satan exists and that he is the author of all evil and suffering, I want to tell you why I believe in God and his unfailing protection and help in the storm.

You are so loved on Earth and in Heaven.

For His Glory and My Good
- Day Three -

"God is our refuge and strength, an

ever-present help in trouble."

~ Psalms 46:1 NIV ~

As I look back on my life, I find so many times that God showed up for me, protected me, and was preparing me for the beautiful plans he has for my life. I think a lot of people could look at my life and find it as proof that God doesn't exist, or at least, that he isn't a good father. But I can confidently say, having lived it, that God has been nothing but a *good, good* father. This next section of my story is heavy. However, there is still hope and beneficial lessons even in my darkest moments, so I pray that if your heart is still hurting and that sensitive topics like these are still painful, that right now, God will be so close to you and heal your scars through the open wounds he stitched up for me.

Like I said in the previous devotional, ever since sin entered the world, evil things are bound to happen. Not because God is sitting in Heaven, orchestrating all of our suffering, but because Satan is trying so futilely to separate us from God, and to keep us from the wonderful life God has in store for us; and if I had given in to the lies Satan had whispered to my heart, I would be dead, and I would never have the opportunity to tell you of God's great love. But I didn't give in. God didn't let me. He fought for me, and now I will fight for him. I pray that my testimony will be another bruise to Satan's head, and another testament to God's existence and love for us.

When I was just a little girl, about six years old, my grandfather, someone whom I trusted and loved very much, began to groom and sexually abuse me. I won't go into the details since they are quite gruesome, but just know that the abuse had lasted for four years and was just about constant. It was hidden from everyone else, and he manipulated me into thinking that if I told anyone, I would be the one in trouble, that it was all my fault. So, naturally, I planned to take it to my grave. I was convinced that my family would hate me if they knew, to the point that I could even imagine their faces twisting in anger and disgust once they found out how dirty my heart truly was. I was just a ten-year-old girl who didn't even know what the word 'molest' meant. I was not to blame, but Satan is good at getting you to believe lies, and now that I'm older and have matured in my relationship with God, I can say beyond a shadow of a doubt that my grandfather was under demonic influence, and his heart and eyes were completely sealed off from God.

In all honesty, there were times I was angry with God, wondering why he would let such a bad thing happen to me; why he wouldn't have protected me from the start. Because of course, Satan's other talent is shifting blame onto God. But just as the Bible promises, God was with me the whole time. He was protecting me. He was giving me courage. He was not forsaking me.

"The Lord Himself goes before you and will be with you; He will never leave you nor forsake you. Do not be afraid; do not be discouraged."
~ Deuteronomy 31:8 NIV ~

Here's how I know the verse above is true:

When I was ten, four years into the abuse, I knew I needed to get out somehow. For the first few years, my grandfather made me believe that what he was doing was normal. But as I was growing up, I quickly realized that no one else in my family was treating me the way he did. It wasn't normal. It wasn't good. I especially realized this when my dear parents began teaching my siblings and me the importance of waiting to have kids in marriage, but here I was, already knowing how kids are made, and knowing that my grandfather wanted to do that with me, too. I'm so thankful the alarms started going off. These red flags were further confirmed when I was traveling with my grandfather to his house in a different city, and for a brief second on the radio before he could change the channel, a news outlet said, "Eleven-year-old girl pregnant, father assumed to be the school janitor." It was so random and out of the blue, but now I know God wanted me to hear it, so I would truly be alerted to the danger coming if I didn't get out now. That's when I started to pray for help.

I grew up in a Christian home, and at the age of five, I prayed to receive God into my heart. I'm unsure if that was truly the day I was saved, but if anything, it was the day I gained head knowledge of God and believed he was real. So I went to him for help. I remember so clearly being curled up on the floor of my shower, crying to God to save me from the abuse. There were times I would tell my grandfather to stop, but it never lasted, and now, I was terrified I would get pregnant. Sadly, at the time, my fear of getting pregnant was mostly because I still thought I was to blame and that God would punish me through pregnancy. I am so thankful that God tore down those lies as well. But after that shower of crying out to God, he filled me with a supernatural peace and courage to face my grandfather. As a short, confident ten-year-old girl, I marched over to his house and told him that he wasn't allowed to touch me ever again; that I wouldn't allow him to hurt me anymore.

That was all God.

My own strength, my own words would have never stopped my grandfather, or Satan who stood next to him, but God could. In that moment, I knew that it was God demanding Satan to get behind me (Matthew 16:23 NIV), because since that day, my grandfather never abused me again, never even brought it up, never even tried to. That was all thanks to God. God saved me when I cried out. God protected me when I trusted that he could help me.

I wish I could say that after the abuse stopped, everything was rainbows and sunshine, but Satan wasn't going to let me get away that easily, especially when he knows the plans God has for me, and the people my story will steal from his grasp. So, almost a year after the abuse ended, the immense stress my body endured from worrying about it starting again and keeping such a painful secret from the people who could help me, my body started to fail, and I was diagnosed with Type 1 Diabetes. At the time, I was still convinced that it was all my fault, and I believed that my diagnosis was the awaited punishment for my sins, because unfortunately, being sexually awakened at a young age makes it easy to fall into further sin, which made me feel like I deserved to be punished. But once again, I cannot stress enough that it wasn't God punishing me and it wasn't God turning his back on me, it was Satan trying to get me to turn my back on God, because even in my diagnosis, God was protecting me.

Before I went to the hospital and was diagnosed, I was losing weight rapidly, and I basically became a shell of myself. I would sit all day in front of our sliding glass door, staring out at nature, as if I were fading away. When my dear Aunt saw me after a period of time, she alerted my parents to how much I had changed and that we should seek medical help; and the crazy thing is, I didn't even think anything was wrong with me.

When my mom called my doctor, they said it sounded like I was going through puberty. When I look back on those days, I truly believe that Satan wanted me to die so that I couldn't complete the work God created me for, but thankfully, my family loved God and was praying for my safety on my behalf. So we decided to skip the appointment scheduled months later and go to the emergency room the next day. That night, my sister said she kept praying for me, fearing that I would die in my sleep, and whenever she would pray, I would roll around in the top bunk, letting her know I was still okay. Thank you, God, for comforting my family, too.

Once we got to the emergency room, everything happened so quickly. With one poke of my finger, the doctors knew I was diabetic, and we were informed that I would be for the rest of my life. Unfortunately, at the time, I was terrified of needles and even said to my mom on the car ride over that as long as they didn't give me a shot, I would be okay, but now I was being told I would be taking multiple shots every day just to live. But once again, God gave me peace that passes all understanding, to the point that I was laughing and smiling with the paramedics during the ambulance ride over. The lady who hooked me up to a heart monitor in the ambulance said I was the happiest person she's ever seen in this circumstance. That was all God.

Of course, the tears did come after a few days in the hospital—and what felt like hundreds of shots later—when we drove down to a bigger children's hospital, and I found out that they had to draw more blood. At that point, I felt like there was no blood left to give, so I cried. But even in this storm, God was still there.

Going back a few days to when I first got to the emergency room, they said my organs were already shutting down, that if we waited even a few hours longer, I would have died. God saved me. God got me the help I needed just in time. God was never trying to punish me or make me go through these horrible things just because I could "handle it." God's perfect will does not include suffering; Satan brought it to us. But have hope, because the Bible promises that God will work everything out for Good.

> *"And we know that in all things God works for the good of those who love him, who have been called according to his purpose."*
> ~ Romans 8:28 NIV ~

Maybe after hearing all of this, you still aren't convinced that God exists or that he loves you. So I want to encourage you to seek him for yourself, and I promise that if you ask in Jesus' name for God to reveal himself to you, he will. Matthew 7:7-8 NIV says,

> *"Ask and it will be given to you; seek and you will find; knock and the door will be opened to you. For everyone who asks receives; the one who seeks finds; and to the one who knocks, the door will be opened."*

You are so loved on Earth and in Heaven.

Seeking Help
- Day Four -

Do not be anxious about anything, but in every

situation, by prayer and petition, with

thanksgiving, present your requests to God.

And the peace of God, which transcends all

understanding, will guard your hearts and your

minds in Christ Jesus."

~ Philippians 4:6-7 NIV ~

After hearing more about my childhood, you
may be wondering what happened next. Did I end up telling anyone? Did I go to the police? Well, this devotional will go in-depth on how I was able to seek help.

To tie the timeline together: first, it was four years of abuse, then I was diagnosed with diabetes, and then a little less than two years later, I was under demonic possession. So, as you can imagine, my mental health was not great, and I was afraid to go to God due to shame and fear from the supernatural encounter, leaving me alone in my suffering. At least, that's what I thought. But even when I wasn't seeking God, others sought him for me, and he remained faithful to me the entire time I avoided him. I am confident of this, solely because everything could have been much worse. Although I began to self-harm, have suicidal thoughts, and was consumed with anger towards my grandfather, wishing God would kill him so I would be safe, God still protected me. He fought against the demons that wanted me dead, stopping me from going too far with harming myself. He shielded me from seeking sexual immorality with other people. Lastly—though there probably is more—he helped me manage my diabetes, and still does. I wasn't alone, but I still didn't know how to ask for help.

I was a Christian at this point in my story, which I believe happened after the demonic possession. That was when my head knowledge of God became a heart knowledge, and though I was scared to go deeper, I knew I needed him as my savior. So, with that said, there were times when I felt the Holy Spirit nudging me to tell someone about what happened. I would either hear a message in church, a devotional, or simply an opportunity that felt right to tell a parent, but I never could. My grandfather drilled it into my head that I was the sinner, that I would be abandoned if they knew. So I continued suffering in silence for about five years after the abuse ended.

When I was fifteen, I was at the end of my rope. My mental health was at its worst. I didn't feel like a normal teenager since I was a diabetic and couldn't eat gluten due to celiac disease, which was a result of my diabetes, and there were so many lies warring in my head at all times. Lies that I was unworthy of love, lies that no one would marry me because of my disease, lies that I was better off dead, lies that God hated me for my sins, lies that I was ugly inside and out, and many more. So when I was at my lowest, I finally cried out to God. I begged him to heal me. At the time, I thought I was asking for healing of my diabetes, but God had plans to heal my heart instead. He's good at knowing what we truly need.

The next day, after watching me deteriorate more and more over the last few months, my mom couldn't stand by and watch me fall apart any longer. So, she asked what was actually going on, because to my family, they thought my only hardship was diabetes; they didn't know the extent of what I was dealing with. I was reluctant to open up, but now I can see that God was guiding my words. Eventually, I said, "I wish I could go back and change things." And my mom, being a good mother, asked, "What would you change?" That's when it all came pouring out. I finally told her everything that happened, and God filled me with a peace that transcended all understanding.

Thankfully, I stayed close to God, and he stayed close to me as we worked with the police, CPS, a therapist, a prosecutor, and others. I knew God was with me in the storm because, for the first time, I found joy again. The lies in my head quieted, and my relationship with my family strengthened; and of course, no one was angry with me for what happened as a child.

Now that you know this part of my story, you may be wondering how this helps you.

I specifically want to talk to the person who feels they are too far gone for God to save—or even want to save them. First of all, that is a lie from Satan. Repeat that to yourself until you believe it. Romans 8:38-39 says that nothing can separate us from God's love. _Nothing_. The angels rejoice in heaven when a sinner comes home, according to Luke 15:7, so I promise that God rejoices when you seek him too. In times of trouble, seek God first; he will help you with the next steps.

Though I don't know your specific circumstances with family and friends, and I unfortunately don't know how they will react to your plea for help, the one thing I do know is that, no matter what anyone tells you, it is not your fault. It is never a child's fault when something evil happens to them. You are blameless. I promise. And even though I don't know how your trusted people will act, God does, that is why seeking him first is so important. He will lead you to the right person at the right time and give you the right words to say. So come home. Let God take on your burdens. Leave the shame at the door and seek help.

You are so loved on Earth and in Heaven.

Through God's Eyes
- Day Five -

"So God created mankind in his own image, in
the image of God he created them; male and
female he created them."
~ Genesis 1:27 NIV ~

Today's topic is one I still have to preach to
myself daily. It is hard to value yourself when you've only
heard lies about how unworthy, useless, ugly, broken, and
dirty you are. But I can promise you that God views us with so
much grace and love that we'll never experience otherwise,
and this gift of love is simply waiting for us to accept it.

When I was a teenager and into adulthood, I had a
consistent feeling that I wasn't good enough for God. I thought
so lowly of myself that it brought me to tears many times. I
hated myself for the habits and sins that stuck from the abuse.
I hated who I became while trying to survive. I hated myself
so deeply that I would chant it over and over to a mirror,
thinking that I needed to live in guilt, shame, and anger for the
rest of my life to atone for the sins I held onto.

I know there is still a long road ahead to reverse the years of constant self-deprecation, but I want to encourage you with what I have learned so far.

"For you created my inmost being; you knit me together in my mother's womb. I praise You because I am fearfully and wonderfully made; Your works are wonderful, I know that fully well."
~ Psalms 139:13-14 NIV ~

As a side note, the song "Wonderfully Made" by Ellie Holcomb has brought me to tears countless times, drowning out the lies lingering in my head with the truths of God's word. So I highly recommend listening to it when you are stuck in a cycle of low self-esteem.

Okay, take a moment to close your eyes and imagine God knitting you in your mother's womb. Imagine him taking his time to create you, a beautiful masterpiece in his own image, for a purpose he will call you to at the appointed time. Imagine God and angels rejoicing when you give your heart to him. Try to fathom that whenever you call out to God, he hears you and will help you, along with everyone else in the entire world who cries out to him (Psalms 34:17). Lastly, remember that God sent his son, the ultimate sacrifice of love, just so he could offer us eternal life in Heaven with him.

Wow.

Don't you feel a little more important now?

I hope so, because it's all true. God does not make mistakes. He created you on purpose because he needed someone just like you to fulfill a calling meant *only* for you.

"For we are God's handiwork, created in
Christ Jesus to do good works, which God
prepared in advance for us to do."
~ Ephesians 2:10 NIV ~

You are not too broken. God will continue to work in your heart to help you grow into the person he calls you to be. Our Father equips us with everything we could ever need (Hebrews 13:20-21) and will walk with us each step of the way.

We usually base something's value on its price, like how most people gravitate towards an expensive item rather than the affordable replica, since we see more value in the higher cost. So what is your value to God? 1 Corinthians 6:20 says that "you were bought at a price." That price was Jesus' life. God's own child was the value he saw in you.

You are so important to God and to the world he created.

I'll say it again.

You are *so* important to the God of the universe, creator of everything, and he did not make even one mistake when creating you. You are wonderfully made in his image.

If you are feeling lost and don't feel like God will ever use you, I encourage you to pray. Ask God to give you peace about the plan he has in store for you. Ask him to reveal the next right step, and I promise he will, in his perfect timing.

You are so loved on Earth and in Heaven.

Sin Keeps Us From God
- Day Six -

"Enter through the narrow gate. For wide is

the gate and broad is the road that leads to

destruction, and many enter through it. But

small is the gate and narrow the road that leads

to life, and only a few find it."

~ Matthew 7:13-14 NIV ~

For many years, I was doing all the motions of

being a Christian. I was going to church, praying, worshipping, talking about God, and so on. But I still felt like Jesus was so far from me.

I worked tirelessly toward the goals God put in my heart. He called me to be an author and to tell my own story when the time was right, so I worked passionately on my writing, hoping it would bring me closer to him. But there was always something in the way.

Sin.

"Surely the arm of the Lord is not too short to

save, nor his ear too dull to hear. But your

I wouldn't say that I was someone who sinned constantly and in many different ways, but there was one big sin that I struggled with due to my abuse. Though it is not easy to admit, since I held so much shame, guilt, and embarrassment about it for years, I had what felt like an incurable addiction to pornography ever since I was about nine years old after my grandfather had shown it to me.

I lived for over a decade in a cycle of sinning, feeling intense guilt, repenting, then going right back to it. I kept excusing it by thinking it wasn't totally my fault, that it was because of the abuse, and that I would never be able to rewire my brain back to purity. I truly, deeply, hated myself because of it. I felt so dirty, claiming to be a Christian, giving others help and advice, yet not being able to defeat my own stronghold. Each time I would fall to sin, Satan would whisper in my ear that it was the last straw, that God couldn't forgive me anymore. I felt so defeated, and whenever I sought out resources for help, I felt even more shame when the only things I found were speaking to men. It felt like I was the only woman in the world who dealt with a pornography addiction, which somehow made me feel even dirtier.

It's just as Paul says,

"For I do not do the good I want to do, but the evil I do not want to do—this I keep on doing."
~ Romans 7:19 NIV ~

That's exactly where I was. I didn't want to sin. I didn't want to keep asking God to help me, then turn around and keep doing the same thing. I was becoming desensitized to sexual immorality, yet becoming hyper-aware of my guilt and shame.

For many years, I thought that's where my story would end. But God is such a good Father that he didn't want me to stay far from him; he wanted me to come home.

Just in the last year, I found a church to call home. As soon as I walked in, I could feel God's presence all around me. It was so beautiful and peaceful that I knew something in my life had to change. I wanted to experience God's presence outside of church too.

This new thirst for God led me to listen to Bryce Crawford, an evangelical podcaster I was introduced to on YouTube. While listening to his messages, a few grabbed my heart and changed my perspective on faith in God. My memory is a little foggy on the exact things said, but two main points stood out to me: one, that the Apostle John uses the phrase "*If* we sin," he does not say when (1 John 2:1-2 NIV), and second, that you're either all in for Jesus, or not at all.

Let me break both of these ideas down further.

Although it is correct that we are born with a sinful nature since we live in a fallen world, meaning we are prone to sinning, Satan deceived me into believing that's all I would ever be. A sinner prone to sinning. But God says that when we accept him into our hearts and the Holy Spirit dwells within us, we are an entirely new creation, and that our old self is gone (2 Corinthians 5:17 NIV). When we become a Christian, God changes our sinful nature to be a nature after Christ's example. So it gave me so much hope to hear that the Bible says, "if" we sin, not "*when*." Because that means with God's help, I *can* live a life without sinning. Jesus' sacrifice gives me that ability. Although it isn't easy—the road is narrow—I have the power, in Christ Jesus, to kill my addiction. I don't have to keep living like a sinner: excusing my sins because I'm human, feeling unworthy of God's forgiveness, and hating myself for my mistakes. I can live like I've been saved: confidently standing before God, knowing he has washed my sins white as snow, learning from my mistakes instead of using them as a weapon, and finally viewing myself as the wonderful creation God says I am.

> *"Submit yourselves, then, to God. Resist the devil, and he will flee from you. Come near to God and He will come near to you. Wash your hands, you sinners, and purify your hearts, you double-minded."*
> ~ James 4:7-8 NIV ~

As for the second statement, I thought that as long as I continued to repent to God, I might still be able to live in the fullness of Christ. But I was so, so wrong. Revelations 3:15-16 NIV says,

> *"I know your deeds, that you are neither cold nor hot. I wish you were either one or the other! So, because you are lukewarm—neither hot nor cold—I am about to spit you out of my mouth."*

Those are some powerful words! It woke me up to the fact that I couldn't just be half-in with God. I had to be all the way in to experience every good thing God promises and to find that peace and joy I so desperately needed.

So with these two revelations in my heart, I began reading the Bible for the first time beyond church or the occasional verse here and there. I read it with a supernatural thirst for more. When I couldn't read it, I would listen to it through an app during work, eight hours each day, wanting to actually learn who God is and who I am in Christ. I was a slave to sin, but the Son of God opened my eyes to the root of the problem and set me free.

"Jesus replied, 'Very truly I tell you, everyone
who sins is a slave to sin. Now a slave has no
permanent place in the family, but a son
belongs to it forever. So if the Son sets you free,
you will be free indeed."
~ John 8:34-36 NIV ~

Once I was supernaturally delivered from my addiction—which I will detail in the next devotional—I was able to fully commit my life to Christ and truly be born again. There is no human language that can properly describe what Jesus did in my heart. He truly made it new. The temptation to sin was completely gone. His presence surrounded me with peace, and he saved me from the path that led to destruction. Shortly after my deliverance, I was able to be baptized along with my husband, and I've never felt so alive until now.

"But because of his great love for us, God, who is rich in mercy, made us alive with Christ even when we were dead in transgressions—it is by grace you have been saved."
~ Ephesians 2:4-5 NIV ~

While I was deep in the sin cycle, I didn't even know what I was missing out on. Only after I gave up the sin and walked the narrow road was I able to realize I was on life support the entire time. When you walk in obedience with God, he will heal your mental scars, give you strength in the fire, and fill you with so much hope for the future. It's not easy, I know, I wrestled with sin for over a decade, but I promise that you have the power in Jesus' name to break down any stronghold keeping you from the beautiful, life-giving gifts God has in store for you. You don't need to keep sinning. You have the power through Jesus to stop the sin cycle. You don't need the addiction. You only need Christ. I promise.

You are so loved on Earth and in Heaven.

The Snake in the Garden
- Day Seven -

"Blessed is the one who perseveres under trial because, having stood the test, that person will receive the crown of life that the Lord has promised to those who love him. When tempted, no one should say, 'God is tempting me.' For God cannot be tempted by evil, nor does he tempt anyone; but each person is tempted when they are dragged away by their own evil desire and enticed. Then, after desire has conceived, it gives birth to sin; and sin, when it is full-grown, gives birth to death."
~ James 1:12-15 NIV ~

In the previous devotional, I said that with God's help, I was able to be completely delivered from my addiction, but I didn't really tell you how that was possible. Throughout my years of knowing God, I believed that sin was always something that we as humans committed because of our sinful nature. I believed that if we just tried hard enough and loved God enough, we would be able to fight sin and flee from temptation. I believed that sin was a war against ourselves. And though there is some truth to that, it's not the whole story.

When Jesus was being tempted in the wilderness before he started his ministry, was it his human nature (since he was fully God and fully man) that was tempting him? No. It was Satan tempting him. Just as I said in the devotional about spiritual warfare, we are not only fighting against our flesh, we are fighting against the devil.

So, I started to view temptation and sin a little differently. I started to view it as the snake in the Garden of Eden, deceiving Eve into eating the fruit. My pornography addiction was not because of my human nature, since I hated it and wanted nothing to do with it when I was in my right mind, but when temptation would come, it was as if a switch in my head flicked, and I obsessively thought about sinning until I did. I wasn't dealing with human nature, no, I was dealing with spiritual forces of evil. Demons.

For some people this may be hard to hear and to accept that we are constantly under attack from the enemy. I mean, it's scary to think about. But unfortunately, it's true. That's why in Ephesians 6:11-17, Paul says to put on the full armor of God for protection against the powers of darkness that want nothing more than to pull us away from God. Keep a ready sword—God's word, the Bible—at all times to fight against the spirits of deception, confusion, temptation, sexual immorality, and every other sin that separates us from God.

So, once I realized I wasn't only fighting my own mind and desires, I learned how to win. As I felt the temptation creeping up and whispering in my ear once more, I declared aloud, "Any evil spirits of sexual immorality flee in Jesus' name. No other spirit aside from the Holy Spirit is allowed in my mind, heart, or home. In Jesus' name, get behind me Satan!"

I haven't heard the whispers of temptations since. It's been over seven months—the longest I had ever gone before in my own strength without sinning was only a few weeks. Praise Jesus!

Now, anytime I feel an inclination to sin, I immediately take it to the Father and declare that any unclean spirits flee in Jesus' name, and the temptation always seems to stop. There is so much power in the name of Jesus. I promise you can be delivered from your cycle of sin as well if you call upon God to vanquish the enemy. Demons have no power in the presence of God.

You are so loved on Earth and in Heaven.

Forgive Yourself
- Day Eight -

*"... Though your sins are like scarlet, they shall
be as white as snow; though they are red as
crimson, they shall be like wool."*
~ Isaiah 1:18 NIV ~

When I was a teenager, I spent so much time
asking for forgiveness from God, then held my mistakes over
myself like a loaded gun. At some point, I was falling to my
addiction so often that it felt like part of the motion to go to
God and ask for his forgiveness, but I didn't believe I deserved
it. I didn't want him to forgive me. I wouldn't let him wash me
white as snow. I thought my sin was a stain that couldn't be
removed, and I constantly reminded myself of that stain. It
made me feel like I deserved every bad thing that happened, it
made me view suffering as my punishment, and it made me
hate myself so much that I would self-harm.

In a world that preached about self-love and learning to
love yourself more, I was so deep in self-loathing that the idea
of loving myself made me sick. I was convinced I didn't
deserve love from anyone, especially from myself. I coped by

blaming myself for every act of sin against me, because somehow that made me feel in control, but in reality, it was controlling me. But imagine this: if God says that for his own sake, he will forget the sins we bring to him in repentance, then why do I keep using them to hurt myself? If the Father forgets, why should I keep reminding him?

"I, even I, am he who blots out your
transgressions, for my own sake, and
remembers your sins no more."
~ Isaiah 43:25 NIV ~

My first step towards healing was not learning to love myself; it was learning to *forgive* myself. This seemingly simple realization changed everything for me. I dug into God's promises and love for us, and everywhere I looked, God was saying I was worthy of forgiveness because of Jesus' sacrifice.

"For as high as the heavens are above the
earth, so great is his love for those who fear
him; as far as the east is from the west, so far
has he removed our transgressions from us."
~ Psalms 103:11-12 NIV ~

The Bible has many verses about forgiving others so that God can forgive you, but I think we can forget that we also need to have that same grace for ourselves so that God can truly wash us white as snow. Though I lived in so much shame and hatred for myself, once God helped me understand I was worthy of forgiveness and that I could also let my mistake go, I felt brand new. I can stand before you now, redeemed. Though it is humbling to admit my mistakes to you all, I'm not ashamed of them anymore; I'm free from them. My mistakes don't hold me back from running into God's arms to receive every good gift he promises.

You can forgive yourself, too.

God's not asking you to remember each and every mistake so that you drown in shame and know "your place." God wants you to learn from your mistakes by changing direction and leaving sin behind, *not* taking it with you. If we don't truly accept the forgiveness offered to us, then Jesus died for nothing. So if you believe that Jesus bore your sin and shame on the cross, then don't let your own unforgiveness be the chains keeping you from God. Don't miss out on the good things God says you are worthy of just because you feel undeserving. He loves you. He forgave you. So take a deep breath, and let the chains fall. Who the Son sets free is free indeed (John 8:34-36 NIV).

You are so loved on Earth and in Heaven.

Bitterness Festers
- Day Nine -

"Be kind and compassionate to one another,
forgiving each other, just as in Christ God
forgave you."
~ Ephesians 4:32 NIV ~

When you grow up in a world that preaches an
eye for an eye and a tooth for a tooth, your own entitlement
begins to take root. Our hearts become vengeful, and we start
to believe that everyone owes us something. But one of the
most deadly poisons in this world is unforgiveness. Bitterness
will fester in your heart until all that's left is an angry,
depressed, and closed-off shell of a person. It's no way to live,
trust me. When I was deep in my anger towards my
grandfather, I became angry at everyone and everything. I was
short-tempered, and the misery in my heart did everything it
could to find company, even if it meant hurting the people I
loved the most. I stopped viewing the world and others
through God's eyes; I viewed them through a lens of hate. But
the most ironic part about letting bitterness take root is that it

doesn't even affect the person who wronged you; it only destroys *you.*

But what does forgiving someone actually look like? For example, if I were to forgive my grandfather, does that mean I have to tell him face-to-face?

No. Not at all. Forgiveness done face-to-face should only be a gift for safe people; people you love, even if they don't seek your forgiveness first. Just one drop of resentment can ruin a relationship that took years to build, so if you care about that person, don't let your pride end it.

The Bible is very clear on the importance of forgiving others so that we may also be forgiven when we repent.

"For if you forgive other people when they sin
against you, your heavenly Father will also
forgive you. But if you do not forgive others
their sins, your Father will not forgive your
sins."
~ Matthew 6:14-15 NIV ~

Or,

"And when you stand praying, if you hold
anything against anyone, forgive them, so that

So if we are to trust in God's Word, does forgiveness mean I act as if nothing happened? Does that mean I allow that person to hurt me again?

Once again, no. Forgiveness does *not* mean you allow an unsafe person back into your life; in fact, they don't even need to know that you forgave them. Forgiving someone breaks the chains of bitterness from your own heart, not theirs. They will have to stand before God and answer for the sins they committed against you, and trust me, our Father is a just God. When we forgive a toxic person, it can be done between you and God—no one else. Let God handle the punishment, don't seek vengeance for yourself, it won't satisfy you as much as giving the hurt to God and being free.

So how do we find the strength to forgive the people who have hurt us so, so badly?

God.

The only way we can let go of bitterness, vengeance, and hate is with God's help. For me, it took many years of crying to God to heal the anger in my heart. I mean, I even prayed for my grandfather to die because I was hurting so much. But as I said earlier, the only one being affected by my hatred was me. It was killing me. It was making me into a person I didn't want to become. Because I wouldn't forgive him, I was allowing what he did to me to still have power over my heart; I was allowing Satan to win.

"... "If your enemy is hungry, feed him; if he is
thirsty, give him something to drink. In doing
this, you will heap burning coals on his head."
Do not be overcome by evil, but overcome evil
with good."
~ Romans 12:20-21 NIV ~

I was done being overcome by evil. So I prayed, "Lord, please heal the bitterness in my heart. Let me have victory over this all-consuming anger. Father, right now, I forgive the evil my grandfather did against me so that I may be set free. Thank you, Jesus. Amen." Peace filled my soul, and joy began to return. To this day, there is no hint of anger towards my grandfather; the only thing that remains is a type of grief for the person he could have been if he had turned to God.

It can be so hard to walk the narrow road; it's easy to stray, but even if it doesn't make sense in the world's eyes, I promise you that the narrow road is filled with so much joy and freedom. Once I removed the unforgiveness in my heart, there was more room for love to grow; there was more capacity to be filled with Jesus' love. I'm so thankful I didn't stay chained in my anger. I encourage you to search your heart for the places where bitterness remains. Once you find them, pray that God will heal them, and, once you are ready, forgive them and be free.

You are so loved on Earth and in Heaven.

Love Is
- Day Ten -

"Love never fails…"

~ 1 Corinthians 13:8 NIV ~

Love is one of the most important themes in the Bible. It is stressed over and over again that if we do not have love, we have nothing. If we do not do everything in love, we have done nothing. Even one of Jesus' greatest commands was to "love each other." (John 13:34-35 NIV) So it's clearly very important to God, but what *is* love? What is this intangible emotion that we throw around loosely and even use when describing tacos? Unfortunately, this fallen world has perverted the meaning of love. Now many people use it as a lie to ensnare others in a cycle of abuse that's labeled as "love." Is that actually love? Or we use the word love—at least in English—to talk about foods we enjoy, movies that entertain us, or activities that bring us happiness. Is that actually love? Was it love when the spouse or friend you had a relationship with for many years stabbed you in the back and left, though countless times they said they loved you? Is that actually love?

"Love is patient, love is kind. It does not envy,
it does not boast, it is not proud. It does not
dishonor others, it is not self-seeking, it is not
easily angered, it keeps no record of wrongs.
Love does not delight in evil but rejoices with
the truth. It always protects, always trusts,
always hopes, always perseveres. Love never
fails..."
~ 1 Corinthians 13:4-8 NIV ~

Love *never* fails. Since love is so important to God, of course, the enemy would pervert it into something meaningless and false. But have hope, because if you look back through your life and wonder, "Was I ever truly loved then?" Here is what God says;

"But God demonstrates his own love for us in
this: While we were still sinners, Christ died for
us."
~ Romans 5:8 NIV ~

God truly *loves* you. He loves us so much that he gave us free will to choose to love him back. He doesn't force us to love him, yet his love never ceases. Since we live in a fallen world, we will experience false love many times, but when humans can't love us as the Bible demonstrates, we can go to God for true love. God does not describe himself as some overarching ruler that created us to be his slaves. On the contrary, God says he is our *Father*, and like a good father, he teaches us, redirects us, and *loves* us. Jesus says that when we follow God's commands, we are no longer servants; we are friends.

> *"Greater love has no one than this; to lay down*
> *one's life for one's friends. You are my friends if*
> *you do what I command. I no longer call you*
> *servants, because a servant does not know his*
> *master's business. Instead, I have called you*
> *friends, for everything I have learned from my*
> *Father I have made known to you."*
> ~ John 15:13-15 NIV ~

That's why the title of this book is: He Leaves the Ninety-Nine. We are God's children, friends, wonderfully made masterpieces, and precious sheep (John 10:11 NIV) that he will continually fight for and protect. Each and every one of us. Now that is love.

So now that we know what love is, what are we
supposed to do with it as followers of Christ?

The Bible makes it very clear that we are supposed to
love in abundance. We are to love our neighbors (other
people) as ourselves. We are to help those in need out of love.
We are to do our best to follow the love described in 1
Corinthians. But how do we do that when people are, well,
people? They can be mean, hurtful, evil, and everything else
under the sun, so why would I want to love them all?

As your relationship with God deepens, our capacity
for love grows as well. Before you know it, you'll be so full of
joy, peace, and love that you can't help but love everything
that God has created, especially those created in his image.
But this only happens when we stop fearing the supernatural

aspects of God—I mean, he did create the whole world, so he's not limited to human understanding—and truly let the Holy Spirit fill us, stretching out our hands to receive any good gift he gives us to use for his kingdom. If we are to believe the Bible, then we know that God is love, and if God is love, then he is everything listed out in 1 Corinthians. He is patient. He is kind. He does not envy, he does not boast, he is not proud. He does not dishonor us, he is not self-seeking, he is not easily angered, and he keeps no record of wrongs. He does not delight in evil but rejoices with the truth. He always protects, trusts, hopes, and perseveres. He never fails us. If that is the God we serve, if that is the God who calls us children, then we have nothing to fear. Our Father gives good gifts, he shows us mercy, and we have the capacity to love because he first loved us.

You are so loved on Earth and in Heaven.

Who is God?
- Day Eleven -

"...Be still, and know that I am God; I will be exalted among the nations, I will be exalted in the earth."

~ Psalms 46:10 NIV ~

When you step outside, feel that gentle breeze, or maybe right now, that pouring rain seeping into the earth to feed all living things. Hear the birds singing a melodious song, or the peaceful quiet in puffy snowflakes floating to the ground. Breathe in the fresh warmth of sunlight, or the richness of a starry sky. Taste the sharp, melting snow in the spring air, or the earthy velvet of autumn. Look around you, trillions of atoms form some of the most beautiful things we could ever imagine. The bubblegum and lavender sky of a winter morning, or the blood orange and lapis lazuli of a summer sun dipping beneath the horizon. The copious flowers blooming in their season, offering medicinal properties or simply a beautiful aroma. A crystal clear lake hiding within it fish that shimmer a rainbow of colors in the sunlight, or jubilant waves kissing the shore, bringing with it swirly shells or even a poisonous sea creature.

When I stand outside, this is what I hear in creation's lullaby: "Be still, and know that I am God." (Psalms 46:10 NIV)

There are too many details, too many wonders for me to believe it all just appeared one day; it had to have a creator. The beginning of Genesis is the only creation story that makes sense to me. It's hard for me to believe it was all a coincidence; it's easy for me to believe that an all-powerful, eternal being created such a beautiful world because of his love for creativity and his desire for fellowship.

So, if I see the world around me and believe there is a God, who is he? Is it Allah? Is it Buddha? Is it the god of the Mormon religion? The Jehovah's Witnesses? Judaism? Or is he the God of the Bible, who sent his son Jesus to bear our sins on the cross so that we may be healed and righteous before God?

"He himself bore our sins in his body on the cross, so that we might die to sins and live for righteousness; by his wounds you have been healed. For you were like sheep going astray,

For me, I chose Jesus, and here's why.

First of all, just about every religion respects Jesus and knows that he was a real person in history. Many of them would also consider him a prophet of God, but the big separation between Christianity and other religions is that they don't believe that Jesus is the Son of God. Of course, that would be the difference, because it's the most important part. John 14:6 NIV says:

"Jesus answered, 'I am the way and the truth and the life. No one comes to the Father except through me."

Or,

"Who is it that overcomes the world? Only the one who believes that Jesus is the Son of God."
~ 1 John 5:5 NIV ~

So if the only way to God is through his son Jesus, then every religion that doesn't believe Jesus is Christ cannot reach God. I feel that it is important to mention—before I go any further—that I believe the Bible points to a trinitarian God, meaning: God the Father is God, Jesus is God, and the Holy Spirit is God. To better understand, I like to think of the Trinity in the context of a human. We are body, soul/mind, and spirit. God is the same way. He is God the Father, Jesus, and the Holy Spirit. One God, three parts, just as we are one human with three parts.

Now, there is one big thing that had to have happened for us to believe that Jesus is the Son of God, therefore we should believe everything he said: He would have had to defeat death.

Many non-Christian sources from the 1st and 2nd centuries confirm Jesus' existence and crucifixion, and we also have eyewitness documentation of his resurrection, dated only a few years after the fact, which is found in 1 Corinthians 15:3-8:

> *"For what I received I passed on to you as of*
> *first importance: that Christ died for our sins*
> *according to the Scriptures, that he was buried,*
> *that he was raised on the third day according to*

the Scriptures, and that he appeared to Cephas,

and then to the Twelve. After that, he appeared

to more than five hundred of the brothers and

sisters at the same time, most of whom are still

living, though some have fallen asleep. Then he

appeared to James, then to all the apostles, and

last of all he appeared to me also…"

Now you might be thinking that using the Bible to prove that Jesus was resurrected on the third day doesn't really count. But imagine this: would you really want to be murdered for a lie that you knew to be a lie? I wouldn't. Yet many people who lived when Jesus did, people throughout history, and even now, are killed for the truth that Jesus is God and that he defeated death.

Maybe you're still not convinced? Then I encourage you to ask God. Say, "God of creation, I believe you exist, but I'm still trying to figure out who you are. Would you please show yourself to me? Would you please help me know if Jesus truly is your son? And if he is, then any spirits of deception or confusion must flee in Jesus' name. Amen." Just try asking, and I know God will hear your request.

Okay, now that I've gone through why I believe there is a God and why I believe the only way to God is through Jesus Christ, now it's time to address why this is even important. Why should you want a relationship with God?

Choosing to follow God is *not* just to secure your spot in Heaven; there is so much more to God than that. His blessings overwhelm us, his love is undeserved but freely given, and his promises are always fulfilled. He is a good God, I promise. But maybe you are still stuck thinking, "If he is a good God, then why does he allow bad things to happen?"

Well, I have a few perspectives I'd like you to consider. Number one, if God did everything the way we wanted him to, the way we thought was best, he wouldn't be God; he would be our puppet. Secondly, since he is God, his ways are higher than our ways (Isaiah 55:8-9 NIV), and everything that was meant for evil against us, God uses it for good.

~ Genesis 50:20 NIV ~

Lastly, as I mentioned before, sin entered the world through Satan and a human's free will. Since we have free will, many people will use their free will to sin against us, and of course, Satan will try his best to destroy us using a fallen world. So, although bad things do happen while living in a fallen world, God promises to hear us, to help us, to love us, and to forgive us.

~ Psalms 103:2-4 NIV ~

The worst thing you could do is have something bad happen because of Satan and then blame God for letting it happen when he's the only one who can help you. But that's exactly what Satan wants you to do. Don't give him a foothold, don't let him win. Instead, run to the God who loves you and wants to heal you physically, situationally, mentally, and spiritually.

You are so loved on Earth and in Heaven.

We Serve a Supernatural God
- Day Twelve -

"For the Spirit God gave us does not make us
timid, but gives us power, love and
self-discipline."
~ 2 Timothy 1:7 NIV ~

For this devotion, I want to challenge your view of God a little bit, but don't worry, this is nothing to be scared of, simply food for thought and prayer.

It's interesting how often we let fear decide for us. It's not easy to resist fear when your mind goes into fight, flight, or freeze for something that might not even be harmful but makes you uncomfortable. I know it all too well. I used to make immediate decisions about God on things that brought a fear of the unknown or dived too deeply into the supernatural because of my past possession, but that is the worst way to make a decision since it totally leaves God out of it and keeps you where you're comfortable. God doesn't ask us to stay comfortable in our faith; instead, the Bible says "Do not be afraid" over one hundred times, depending on the translation.

So I think it's safe to say that we shouldn't be afraid of God's supernatural state of being.

Before I go any further, I want to make sure we are on the same page with what supernatural even means, which in basic terms is: *something that goes beyond scientific understanding.* So when I say God is a supernatural God, I don't mean anything scary that is usually associated with that term. I just mean he goes beyond mere human understanding, which I'm assuming we can all agree on since he created the entire world with just his words.

Alright, now that we are on the same page, dive deeper with me. In this devotion, I will mainly be speaking to people who have already put their faith in Jesus and believe in the Bible, but I think this lesson can still be beneficial for anyone, so please pray for God to give you discernment, and do not be afraid.

So, we believe that God spoke to a man named Noah, and had him build a ginormous ark over many decades, then God sent a male and female of each animal species to just show up and enter the ark, then God flooded the entire world to wipe out the great evil that filled the Earth, and finally, he created a beautiful rainbow as his promise never to flood the whole Earth again. Believable, right?

Because we believe in the Bible, we believe that Samson had super strength until they cut his hair, we believe that a pit of hungry lions didn't eat Daniel, we believe that Jesus died but didn't stay that way, we believe that Jonah was swallowed by a great fish, perhaps a whale, and then spit back out after three days, we believe that the Holy Spirit was able to allow people to speak a different language either of men or of angels, we believe that Moses split the Red Sea so that his people could cross it on dry ground, we believe in the ten plagues of Egypt, and so many more historical events that can feel more like fiction than reality. So why do we believe they happened?

Well, the answer is simple. There is a common denominator in all of these stories that makes everything possible: God. Samson wasn't Superman, Daniel wasn't a lion whisperer, and Moses' staff wasn't some magical wand. They served a supernatural God who gave them the ability to perform supernatural miracles. Christians like to repeat the verse, *"I can do all this through him who gives me strength"* (Philippians 4:13 NIV), but once it gets too supernatural, we let fear say, "God doesn't do that anymore." But why not? Why can't a supernatural God continue to do supernatural things for his kingdom? Why are we putting him in the box of what we are comfortable with? Just think, every scary and freaky thing we see demons do, God could easily do as well, and the only reason he doesn't is either that it is evil, or, since we have free will, we don't let him. This is the big difference between God and Satan: Satan doesn't need permission if you've left the door open for him to walk through, whereas God stands at the door and knocks (Revelation 3:20 NIV). So it's unwise to think that God is not at least as powerful as Satan's little henchmen.

A good majority of Christians believe that the gifts of the Holy Spirit were only for the first century, and once again, I think that's putting God in a box, and here's why: if it's to advance his kingdom, why wouldn't he give good gifts through the Advocate to help us? Paul says these gifts will cease when completeness comes (1 Corinthians 12:8-12), and personally, I have always believed that we are only made whole and complete when we are in Heaven, face-to-face with God, not while we are still on Earth. With all of that said, I understand and can relate to feeling uncomfortable with things that go beyond our understanding—I mean, we are just humans—so I encourage you not to just take my word for it, and to pray for discernment and to sincerely ask God if his gifts are still available to you. I have faith he will answer your questions, even if they are brought to him in fear.

To wrap this up with a nice bow: don't be surprised if God, the creator of *everything*, still uses supernatural things to advance his kingdom. It's also good to remember that this topic doesn't affect your salvation. It is minor theology, so don't be afraid to wrestle with it.

You are so loved on Earth and in Heaven.

Sharpen Your Sword
- Day Thirteen -

"For the word of God is alive and active.
Sharper than any double-edged sword, it
penetrates even to dividing soul and spirit,
joints and marrow; it judges the thoughts and
attitudes of the heart."
~ Hebrews 4:12 NIV ~

For most of my walk with Christ, I barely read the Bible. I always found it hard to understand, and—I'm so sorry, Lord—boring. I didn't see why I needed to be in the Word as much as possible; I thought I got my fill at church on Sunday. Boy, was I wrong! The more time you spend in God's Word, the more you begin to imitate it. You reflect its joy, its peace, its love, and its teachings. So, how do we read it more? How does something boring become our favorite book? Here are some things that helped me.

For starters, I grew up owning a *KJV* (*King James Version*) Bible, which only made it harder for me to read since it is written in early modern English. If you thrive with this translation, then please continue to use it, but for me, I needed

77

a Bible in the *current* modern English, the language I speak and can easily comprehend. So don't feel ashamed if you grew up on the *KJV* and need to switch to better understand it. I've learned that there is no *one* right translation; most of them are still God's word, so don't be afraid to find the version that feels right to you through prayer and discernment with God. So, all that to say, I now read the NIV (New International Version), and I find it much more immersive.

The next thing that helped me a lot is listening to an audio Bible. I have always struggled with reading non-fiction, so whenever I would read the Word, my mind would keep wandering, and I'd have to read one simple verse over and over again for it to actually take root in my heart. But I love listening to podcasts. So, I thought I'd try listening to the Bible, and I purchased the *Dwell* app. In only a few weeks, I had pretty much listened to the whole Bible, was genuinely fascinated by the stories in the Old Testament, and was brought to tears by Jesus' life in the New Testament. It was so beautiful to hear it and have it go straight to my heart rather than being stuck processing in my brain for ten million hours! So if you struggle to stay focused, or you simply don't have much time to sit and read, I highly suggest finding an audio Bible you like to help you soak in so much more of God's Word.

Okay, I'm guessing some people still aren't convinced of the Bible's importance in their life—I should know, it took me almost two decades to overcome—so now I want to lay out some reasons why, along with prayer, it is the most important part of your walk with Christ.

"But in your hearts revere Christ as Lord.
Always be prepared to give an answer to
everyone who asks you to give the reason for
the hope that you have. But do this with
gentleness and respect."
~ 1 Peter 3:15 NIV ~

Do you know what you believe? I've found it very hard to share my faith when I had no confidence in the foundation of my faith. As Peter says, we need to always be prepared to share our faith, and for years, I would simply listen to other religious beliefs and say nothing since I didn't know how to defend my own. Trust me, that is no way to walk with God. But once I started listening to and reading God's Word, I found so much more confidence and a deep respect for the faith I cling to. Now, I feel ready to share my faith—hence why I'm writing this devotional—and I'm actually excited to share it. What's even more awesome is that when I share my testimony now, verses will just come flooding in from the Holy Spirit since I've been "sharpening my sword" (God is so cool). So, I encourage you, sharpen your sword, and as Joshua says:

"Keep this Book of the Law always on your lips; meditate on it day and night, so that you may be careful to do everything written in it. Then you will be prosperous and successful."
~ Joshua 1:8 NIV ~

There is nothing like the peace that comes from dwelling in God's Word. When I was deep into my mental health spirals, the only things that would help were worship music and reading the Bible. I would just flip to Psalms and force myself to start reading, and instantly, the anger that caused a triggered response would melt away, and I would weep in God's presence until I was okay again.

"Your word is a lamp for my feet, a light on my path."
~ Psalms 119:105 NIV ~

Trust me, I know it's hard to start reading the Bible, but once you find your method, you won't want to go back. You will find yourself wanting more and more of it, and naturally, you will feel even closer to God's heart. Maybe don't start in Genesis for the millionth time; try starting with Matthew, or Psalms, or in one of my current favorites, Ephesians or James. You don't have to start at the beginning; start where you will feel most edified, and if you feel too overwhelmed by all 66 choices, pray. God will be faithful and happy to help you know where to start.

The first part of this chapter was mostly geared towards Christians who have accepted the Bible as God's Word, but now I want to talk to the person who denies that it is God-inspired. To start, I agree with you that humans can make mistakes, and the fact that the Bible was written by humans, preserved by humans, and translated by humans over two thousand years, makes it hard to completely trust that what we have now is exactly what God intended.

But before I go into detail about my opinion on that statement, I think it's important to point out the obvious fact that this was written over *two thousand years ago*. That means the culture, worldviews, and the things people innately knew and understood were all different from how we operate today.

So if you read something in the Bible that makes no sense in today's context, first pray for wisdom from the Holy Spirit, and second, research the culture of that time. Maybe in that year, there were cultural practices that weren't in God's perfect will, but they still happened and were still documented. The Bible is full of imperfect and broken people; it's not filled with perfect examples of who God wants you to be.

Okay, now that I've hopefully made that point clear, I will go into my suggestion for addressing the claim above. Yes, there is a good chance the Bible was/is affected by human error—I mean, everything I do, even with God's help, is affected by human error. So what do we do? Do we throw out the whole Bible and say it's not from God? No. A good portion of the Bible is simply historical accounts that can be verified, and I don't see anything harmful in reading history. Actually, scholars widely accept that the Bible has been preserved with a high degree of accuracy because it is an "open transmission." Meaning, rather than one copy being preserved for hundreds of years, thousands of copies have been created throughout history that say basically the same thing.

Next, I always, always suggest praying before reading the Bible to gain wisdom and discernment as you read. Before I have a "religion," I have a relationship with God, so the most important thing is to listen to what he reveals to me rather than my own understanding.

> *"If any of you lacks wisdom, you should ask*
> *God, who gives generously to all without*
> *finding fault, and it will be given to you."*
> ~ James 1:5 NIV ~

Lastly, over anything else you read in the Bible, I have come to believe that the most important piece to build your faith and life on is Jesus. He is our example and direct connection to God. So even if you don't believe the Bible is inspired by God, you can cling to the historical records of Jesus' life to build your faith. As a Christian, everything for me goes back to Jesus, so I build everything on the foundation of his example.

You are so loved on Earth and in Heaven.

Death Spiral
- Day Fourteen -

"Do not conform to the pattern of this world,
but be transformed by the renewing of your
mind. Then you will be able to test and approve
what God's will is—His good, pleasing and
perfect will."
~ Romans 12:2 NIV ~

Evil is all around us. It's in our media, entertainment, government (no matter who is in office), and it's
everywhere you look. It can feel so overwhelming and
suffocating to live in a fallen world. But as Christians, our
hope is in Christ, who has already won.

"But thanks be to God! He gives us the victory
through our Lord Jesus Christ."
~ 1 Corinthians 15:57 NIV ~

But how do we protect ourselves while here on Earth?
First of all, we wear the armor of God! (Ephesians 6:10-17)
Don't just read the verse and imagine putting armor on (I may,

or may not be guilty of this…). Live it out! You buckle the belt of truth by being honest, loving truth, and seeking it. The breastplate of righteousness is worn by being in right standing with God; leave your sins at the foot of the cross and live a life after God's own heart. The shoes of the gospel of peace are slipped on when you are slow to anger, bountiful in grace, and bring peace wherever you go, spreading the gospel with love. Your shield of faith can only protect you when you spend time with God, you understand what you believe, and you have faith in God's promises. The helmet of salvation is equipped when you anchor your thoughts on Christ and don't let doubts take root, making you turn from God; instead, address them immediately with the Bible and your Christian brothers and sisters. Lastly, sharpen your sword! A rusty, chipped sword will do no good against this evil world, so sharpen and hone your sword of the Spirit so you are prepared for anything. The armor of God is not something you "wear", it's something you have to act out—it's how you should live your life.

Next, discernment is so, so important. Don't just listen to a song because it sounds cool, don't just watch a show because it's popular, don't follow a new trend because your favorite YouTuber does, actually take the time to look into the meaning, names, and themes behind all of these things. Be aware of the things you feed your mind because it will influence your heart in either a good or bad way.

There is power in names. That's why Jesus changed Saul's name to Paul and Simon's name to Peter. We know there's power in the name of Jesus, so it's only wise to assume that other names hold power too. So, I encourage you to look into names and understand what they mean. For example, there was a metal band that I loved listening to whose name raised a red flag, but I quickly dismissed it, thinking it didn't matter. But when I started paying closer attention to names and looked them up, I was disturbed to learn that the name is an actual device used to hear spiritual entities (demons) in recordings. I *immediately* deleted all of their songs. I'm not taking any chances! That band was "Spiritbox," by the way. Another example was when I looked up song titles I didn't understand from another band I listened to, and learned that they were the actual names of demons. Now, if I don't know what something means, I don't ignore it; I take a moment to understand it.

This next topic is more specific to the ladies, but could still be useful for anyone. I hate to say it, but smut is sexual immorality! (Trust me, I'm speaking to myself for this one since I let a lot slide in the books I was reading in the past.)

"Flee from sexual immorality. All other sins a person commits are outside the body, but whoever sins sexually, sins against their own body. Do you not know that your bodies are temples of the Holy Spirit, who is in you, whom you have received from God? ... Therefore honor God with your bodies."
~ 1 Corinthians 6:18-20 NIV ~

I know that it is hard to find clean, well-written love stories, but it is so worth it to be picky and not read the popular book that will cause you to sin. This lack of clean stories is why I'm becoming an author (Sorry for the shameless plug.) I want to publish books that have all the giddy, feet-kicking romance without the sexual immorality that's basically erotica but labeled as a "rom-com." I'm writing these stories to bring glory to God and to use the gifts he has given me as he has instructed. I hope you'll check them out! The Heartening Series will be the quintessential high school rom-com, following a large cast of characters from 11th grade through college on their journey with God. The Fate Series is my own twist on legends and myths, so that people can have versions of these fairytales that aren't tied to demonic entities, and of course, there is romance. (End of shameless plug. Thanks for reading.) Now, maybe you are wondering why sexual immorality is something you should be so adamant in avoiding, especially when it's so normalized and labeled as "liberation" or "freedom." Well, I can tell you right now that it is not freeing or liberating. In fact, I have found in my research that sexual immorality is one of the main causes for spiritual attacks and letting demonic influence into your life—that's one of the reasons why evil people created a thing called sex magic, using it to summon demons. So trust me, it is so, so dangerous, and not worth it AT ALL.

As far as TV goes, we can become so desensitized to evil, killing, sexual immorality, drunkenness, foul language, etcetera, just from what we watch. So be picky! You'll be surprised when you start looking that there is a lot of good, wholesome entertainment that isn't strictly from a religious source, so don't worry about being forced to give up every type of entertainment; just use discernment when trying something new.

*"The eye is the lamp of the body. If your eyes
are healthy, your whole body will be full of*

light. But if your eyes are unhealthy, your
whole body will be full of darkness…"
~ Matthew 6:22 NIV ~

If you start intentionally looking, you will find demonic influence/symbolism everywhere. I don't say this to scare you; I say this to make you aware. For instance, look into the origins of yoga and how it's used to worship Hindu gods and become one with the divine. Look into zodiac signs and what they mean in astrology, and how they use the celestial bodies to predict divine omens which the Bible implicitly speaks against—read Deuteronomy 4:19, Deuteronomy 18:10-12, and the second half of Leviticus 19:26. Look into angel numbers before you just get one tattooed on your skin since they are a part of numerology and consider them as encouragement from a spirit guide—I find it especially unnerving that 666 is one of these "angel number," or that all the numbers are repeating, synchronized numbers just like the mark of the beast talked about in Revelations. Look into the seal of Solomon and what it means and where it's used—you can't convince me that the star of David is not just the seal of Solomon since the seal of Solomon came first. Look into what drugs and a state of drunkenness can bring about. For instance, why are there so many reports of people using Ayahuasca or DMT seeing serpent entities? Weird, right? Must be why the Bible instructs us to be of a sober mind. Another symbol that I totally missed and didn't think much of (for some reason) is the Hellfire Club in Stranger Things. I just thought it was a made up name to sound scary or tough. But, with a simple internet search, you can see that the Hellfire Club is actually a real club that was created to mock Christianity. Here I was not thinking much about why all of the Stranger Things merchandise has the Hellfire Club symbol on it, which is literally a depiction of the devil. Oh boy, was I blind to a lot of things. Not that any of these rabbit holes are fun and hope-bringing things to explore, I still think it is important to be aware of what's going on around you.

When we follow the way of the world and the things it says we should like, we end up in a death spiral. If you've never heard of that term before, it is a phenomenon that occurs when blind ants get separated from the main colony and follow the scent of the ant in front of them, ultimately trapping themselves in an endless loop until the very last ant is dead from starvation. Pretty intense, huh? Well, that's exactly what happens when we lose sight of God and follow the masses. We are called to be set apart (1 Peter 2:9 NIV), not so that we can boast about ourselves, but to be saved from destroying ourselves. So don't follow the masses in a blind death spiral; follow Christ on the narrow road that leads to life.

Don't give Satan a foothold in your life with the things you ignorantly let in. But have hope, because where there is evil, there is also good. There are hundreds of beautiful testimonies of people finding and experiencing the true God in miraculous ways. Also, God promises to protect us and give us peace in the storm. So do not be afraid; the demons tremble at the name of Jesus.

You are so loved on Earth and in Heaven.

A Letter from God
- Day Fifteen -

"But grow in the grace and knowledge of our Lord and Savior Jesus Christ. To him be glory both now and forever! Amen."
~ 2 Peter 3:18 NIV ~

God is not the earthly father who hurt you; he is not the boss who does not value you; he is not the stranger who passed you by; he is your creator. He made you on purpose and loves you beyond measure.

Maybe right now, all you feel towards God is hate, anger, or confusion. Maybe you've decided in your heart that there is no God because he wasn't there when you needed him to be. But how do you know he wasn't there? What if what you were experiencing, no matter how horrible, was the rain, and he was holding back the storm? How can we possibly know all the things that could've happened? During my years of addiction, there were countless times I asked God to heal me so I wouldn't have to live in corrosive, all-consuming shame any longer. So why didn't he answer? Why did he wait for over a decade? No. Those are the wrong questions to ask.

Why didn't I believe he *could* heal me?

"Daughter, your faith has healed you. Go in peace and be freed from your suffering."
~ Mark 5:34 NIV ~

"Therefore I tell you, whatever you ask for in prayer, believe that you have received it, and it will be yours."
~ Mark 11:24 NIV ~

Why was there a part of me that *didn't* want to stop?

"As a dog returns to its vomit, so fools repeat their folly."
~ Proverbs 26:11 NIV ~

"For in my inner being I delight in God's law; but I see another law at work in me, waging war against the law of my mind and making me a prisoner of the law of sin at work within me. What a wretched man I am! Who will rescue me from this body that is subject to death? Thanks be to God, who delivers me through Jesus Christ our Lord!"

~ Romans 7:22-25 NIV ~

Why did I believe I *deserved* to feel guilt and shame, making me think I *shouldn't* be free from it?

"For I take no pleasure in the death of anyone, declares the Sovereign Lord. Repent and live!"
~ Ezekiel 18:32 NIV ~

"He himself bore our sins in his body on the cross, so that we might die to sins and live for righteousness; by his wounds you have been healed."
~ 1 Peter 2:24 NIV ~

Why did *I* try to defeat it all on my own?

"I am the vine; you are the branches. If you remain in me and I in you, you will bear much fruit; apart from me you can do nothing."
~ John 15:5 NIV ~

*"Unless the Lord builds the house, the builders
labor in vain. Unless the Lord watches over the
city, the guards stand watch in vain."*
~ Psalms 127:1 NIV ~

So maybe it wasn't that God didn't show up for you.
Maybe you didn't let him. Maybe you didn't have faith that he
would. Maybe you, deep down, didn't want to be helped.
Maybe you thought you could do it all on your own. Maybe
you went right to blaming, doubting, and hating him before he
could even show up. God is not *punishing* you. His
redirections are kind, not devastating. He is not an
authoritarian, arbitrary God. He is the God who hears you and
loves you. He sees our struggles and does not turn a blind eye.

*"She gave this name to the Lord who spoke to
her: "You are the God who sees me,"..."*
~ Genesis 16:13 NIV ~

I think it is important to remember that, although
nothing can separate us from God's *love* (Romans 8:38-39
NIV). We can be separated from *God* (Isaiah 59:1-2 NIV). Just
as Jesus says in Matthew 10:25-30 NIV, there is no external
force that can snatch us from God's hand, but 2 Chronicles

15:2 NIV says: *"... The Lord is with you when you are with him. If you seek him, he will be found by you, but if you forsake him, he will forsake you."* I am not one to believe that after being saved, if you later reject God, you are guaranteed salvation in the end. Paul says in 1 Timothy 4:1 NIV: *"The Spirit clearly says that in later times some will abandon the faith and follow deceiving spirits and things taught by demons."* I think abandoning the "faith" is the big takeaway from this verse. Through my research of the Bible, I have come to believe that if you fully reject God, he will leave. He will never stop loving you, but he will respect your choice to abandon your faith in him. I mean, faith in him is the only way to be saved, according to Paul.

> *"If you declare with your mouth, 'Jesus is*
> *Lord,' and believe in your heart that God*
> *raised him from the dead, you will be saved.*
> *For it is with your heart that you believe and*
> *are justified, and it is with your mouth that you*
> *profess your faith and are saved."*
> ~ Romans 10:9-11 NIV ~

When I look back on my story, I can see the different stages of faith that I went through. When I was five years old,

I had a head-knowledge of God. I could declare with my mouth that Jesus is Lord, but it took an experience like being possessed to believe it in my heart. That's when I had a heart-knowledge of God and was saved. But that isn't the last stage. I spent over a decade wrestling with my sin, finding faith in God to be hard, and wanting just to avoid the whole topic of religion altogether. It took stepping into the presence of God again at my new church to see how desperately I needed a savior. I needed Jesus, all of him, not just the parts of him that were easy. In September 2025, I gave my life to Christ, *fully*. I let go of the sins that were separating me from his presence, I let go of the misconception that he was punishing me, and I accepted the complete salvation only Jesus can offer. I was washed clean. I was renewed. And I am *never* going back. When you truly experience God, the supernatural, true God of creation, there is no going back. He has done miracles in my life by breaking an addiction that lasted over a decade, breaking a bad habit of biting my nails that I've had since I was a little child, taking away the panic attacks and self-harm I was committing, answering prayers in miraculous ways through instantly healing my sicknesses, providing 150 units of insulin from my last vial that only had drops in it, blessing Noah and me in ways that have brought me to tears, giving me gifts of the Holy Spirit, and so, so much more. I can confidently say he is a good, good God.

But with all of that said, I know that I am still growing and learning. My faith will continue to strengthen, and God will continue to reveal new truths to me. Lately, I've loved digging deeper into the history of my faith, and one of my favorite things to do has been wrestling with theological topics. So I am nowhere near the end of my journey. I can't wait to see what God does!

I've always enjoyed the "Jesus Calling" devotionals, so these are the words—through much prayer and waiting—God has put in my heart for you. I pray you receive them, and I pray that you go back to your searching shepherd and find community and home with the ninety-nine.

Be still and know that I am God. I am with you in the storm, I am with you in the fire, and I am with you in the darkness. I will be your safety, I will be your protection, and I will be your light. You are my child, and I am your Father, and you are worth dying for. You are a necessary part of my creation, and when I look at you, I see that you are good.

My love is all around you. My love is in the pleasant breeze, my love is in the warm sunlight on your skin, my love is in the ocean waves, my love is in the wildflowers, my love is in all of creation; find my signature there. But although I love you so much and I want to help and guide you, I will wait for you to love me back; I will wait for you to ask. You don't have to be lost with no hope for the future. Come to me and find your rest. You are always welcome home with open arms and a celebration for your return. But until then, I am always near, just ask in faith, and I will hear your cry.

*"The Lord bless you and keep you; the Lord
make his face shine on you and be gracious to
you; the Lord turn his face toward you and give
you peace."*
~ Numbers 6:24-26 NIV ~

You are so loved by the Father in Heaven who created you, loves you, and is waiting for you.

Dear God,

I pray that you will use this devotional to reach the heart of stone and turn it back to flesh. I pray that you will meet this dear reader where they are, but not leave them there. I pray that you would reveal yourself to them in a supernatural and undeniable way so that they may find the fountain of life pouring from your love. Thank you, Jesus, for your perfect and holy sacrifice that enables us to stand before God, washed clean of sins. Our sins had a cost; thank you for paying it. Lord Jesus, I pray that you would lovingly motivate this dear reader to seek you once more and leave their burdens, sins, and pain at the foot of the cross. Your will be done, Father, on Earth as it is in Heaven. In *Jesus* name, amen.

What's Next?
- Resources -

What's next? Maybe after reading this devo-
tional, you are wanting to dive deeper into your faith. If so, here are some resources that have helped my own journey of searching. All the resources (except the app) are available on YouTube or your favorite podcast app. Also, please keep an eye out for more devotionals coming soon! The next one I am writing is *A Daughter of God,* which is filled with the lessons I've learned while walking with Christ. Topics like marriage, community, prayer, etcetera. I'm also working on one called *My Doubtful Heart* that focuses on the big stuff, like: where did Satan come from, why do good people go to hell, what are angels, and some ideas I have been wrestling with. I hope you'll look forward to reading them all!

Disclaimer: Just like anything else you listen to and absorb, please use discernment and pray about anything that doesn't feel right in your spirit. These fellow brothers in Christ are also human, so give them grace.

1. Bryce Crawford Podcast

   Bryce has really challenged my faith in God and
   helped me thirst for more knowledge of what I
   believe. My heart would not have been changed if it
   were not for listening to this young man's wisdom.

2. Haunted Cosmos Podcast

   Two men of God, Ben and Brian, who are genuinely
   so funny yet poetic. They both have helped me gain
   spiritual discernment, understand the enemy, and find
   the courage to go deeper with God.

3. Johnny Chang

   Johnny's knowledge and wisdom about God and the
   Bible have helped me understand my faith
   tremendously. Also, his testimony is so powerful,
   and he shares it with such a genuine heart.

4. Dwell App (Audio Bible)

   I've loved using this app to listen to God's word
   when I am at work, driving, first waking up, and any
   other time when I can't sit and physically read it.

Battle Armor
- Playlist -

1. Wonderfully Made - Ellie Holcomb
2. Same God - Hannah Kerr
3. Heaven's Eyes - Jillian Edwards
4. It's Always Been You - Phil Wickham
5. Holy Spirit - Francesca Battistelli
6. IN THE ROOM - Forrest Frank
7. Good to Me - Audrey Assad
8. Cloud And Fire - Josiah Queen
9. Not in a Hurry - Will Reagan & United Pursuit
10. You Say - Loren Allred
11. Made For More (Studio Version) - Josh Baldwin
12. It Is So - Elevation Worship
13. Homecoming - Bethel Music, Cory Asbury & Gable Price
14. Abandoned - Benjamin William Hastings & Brandon Lake
15. Already Done - Free Worship

Author Note

- Closing -

This whole devotional has basically been one big author note, so I will keep it short. Thank you so much for taking the time to read my story. I am very humbled to share it with you, and in all honesty, there are a few parts I wish I could tear out! But I know God has redeemed those parts of my story, so I am not ashamed, only humbled.

I thought I would have quite a few more years of growth and experience before I shared my testimony, but God asked me to write this devotional much sooner than expected. So, although I don't feel like the most qualified person to share my opinions, in the end, they are *my* opinions, formed with God's help. More than anything, I hope you will do your own research, prayer, and digging into these topics to form your own opinions, and I would love to hear your thoughts! I love challenging my faith in a respectful and beneficial way, so please email me, message me on Instagram, or if you have my number, send me a text! I want to know your thoughts.

I pray that through my story, you won't feel so alone in your struggles after reading my own. I was so blessed while writing this book, and I found even more healing as I recounted the grace God has shown me and the lessons he's blessed me with.

This devotional is my flaming arrow at Satan's kingdom! Lord, let it take fire, and light the path that leads your children home.

@blujaay_the_writer

Grace Hockin is a Christian author from Michigan who focuses on bringing God into classic stories, such as the quintessential rom-com, the highly popular romantasy genre, psychological thrillers, and more. Her first published work is the non-fiction *He Leaves the Ninety-Nine*, an intimate account of her life in devotional form, reminiscing about the times God has intervened in miraculous ways. Aside from being a writer, Grace is a self-proclaimed hobby hoarder, a wife, and a coffee shop enthusiast. She can be reached at: gracewrites2001@gmail.com.

Coming Soon!

THE HeARTening SERieS: BOOK ONE
BATTLING FOR
YOUR HEART
A NOVEL
GRACE HOCKIN
MOLLY WEIDENFELLER

The Fate Series: Book One
A Losing Game of
Fate
A Novel
Grace Hockin
Molly Weidenfeller

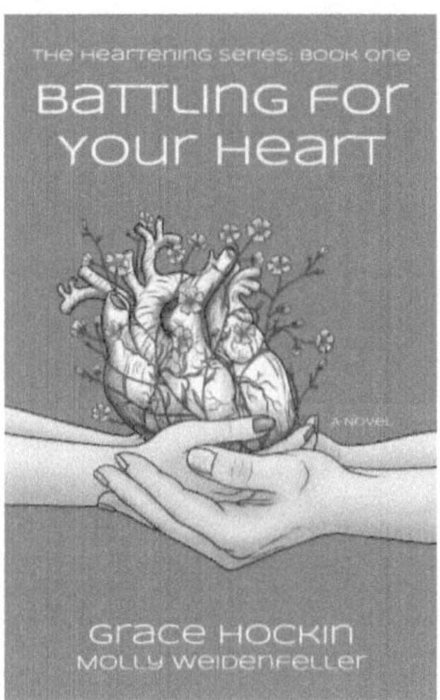